Editor-in-Chief and Founder:
 Lyndon H. LaRouche, Jr.
Editorial Board: *Lyndon H. LaRouche, Jr. , Helga
 Zepp-LaRouche, Robert Ingraham, Tony
 Papert, Gerald Rose, Dennis Small, Jeffrey
 Steinberg, William Wertz*
Co-Editors: *Robert Ingraham, Tony Papert*
Managing Editor: *Nancy Spannaus*
Technology: *Marsha Freeman*
Books: *Katherine Notley*
Ebooks: *Richard Burden*
Graphics: *Alan Yue*
Photos: *Stuart Lewis*
Circulation Manager: *Stanley Ezrol*

INTELLIGENCE DIRECTORS
Counterintelligence: *Jeffrey Steinberg, Michele
 Steinberg*
Economics: *John Hoefle, Marcia Merry Baker,
 Paul Gallagher*
History: *Anton Chaitkin*
Ibero-America: *Dennis Small*
Russia and Eastern Europe: *Rachel Douglas*
United States: *Debra Freeman*

INTERNATIONAL BUREAUS
Bogotá: *Miriam Redondo*
Berlin: *Rainer Apel*
Copenhagen: *Tom Gillesberg*
Houston: *Harley Schlanger*
Lima: *Sara Madueño*
Melbourne: *Robert Barwick*
Mexico City: *Gerardo Castilleja Chávez*
New Delhi: *Ramtanu Maitra*
Paris: *Christine Bierre*
Stockholm: *Ulf Sandmark*
United Nations, N.Y.C.: *Leni Rubinstein*
Washington, D.C.: *William Jones*
Wiesbaden: *Göran Haglund*

ON THE WEB
e-mail: eirns@larouchepub.com
www.larouchepub.com
www.executiveintelligencereview.com
www.larouchepub.com/eiw
Webmaster: *John Sigerson*
Assistant Webmaster: *George Hollis*
Editor, Arabic-language edition: *Hussein Askary*

EIR (ISSN 0273-6314) *is published weekly
(50 issues), by EIR News Service, Inc.,
P.O. Box 17390, Washington, D.C. 20041-0390.
(703) 777-9451 ext. 415*

European Headquarters: E.I.R. GmbH, Postfach
Bahnstrasse 9a, D-65205, Wiesbaden, Germany
Tel: 49-611-73650
Homepage: http://www.eirna.com
e-mail: eirna@eirna.com
Director: Georg Neudecker

Montreal, Canada: 514-461-1557

Denmark: EIR - Danmark, Sankt Knuds Vej 11,
basement left, DK-1903 Frederiksberg, Denmark.
Tel.: +45 35 43 60 40, Fax: +45 35 43 87 57. e-mail:
eirdk@hotmail.com.

Mexico City: EIR, Sor Juana Inés de la Cruz 242-2
Col. Agricultura C.P. 11360
Delegación M. Hidalgo, México D.F.
Tel. (5525) 5318-2301
eirmexico@gmail.com

The Role of the Individual in History Today

EIRContents

www.larouchepub.com Volume 43, Number 35, August 26, 2016

Cover This Week

Alfred Herrhausen

Econ Taschenbuch Verlag

I. Critical September Days

How We Will Create a New Financial Architecture

by David Christie, LaRouche PAC Policy Committee

Aug. 23—The Berlin Wall was not demolished as the result of the success of an election campaign. Nor was it a referendum which brought hundreds of thousands into the streets to ultimately smash through concrete and rebar—to see their family and friends they had been partitioned from for decades. The Berlin Wall came down for the reasons that Lyndon LaRouche had identified in his speech at the Kempinski Hotel in Berlin a little over a year before the wall fell—the intellectual, cultural and economic mortar of that society could no longer sustain and nourish its population.

The state of society within the trans-Atlantic community is far worse today than that of Germany in 1989. The structural integrity of our own wall degenerated long ago, and either it will come down by financial collapse and world war, or we will embrace what is on the other side: the growing New Paradigm spreading throughout Eurasia. At the core of this new paradigm is the "New Silk Road" concept, put forward by Lyndon LaRouche and his wife Helga Zepp-LaRouche 25 years ago, as well as the extraordinary space program that is coming into increasing focus around China's declared mission to land on the far side of the moon by 2018.

However, there is no way this new paradigm can be realized without a new financial architecture to facilitate its growth. From his call for the creation of an "International Development Bank" in 1975, to his more recent proposal for the convening of a "New Bretton Woods Conference," Lyndon LaRouche has repeatedly proven that the creation of a new global "financial architecture" is a prerequisite for the development of a new world-wide physical economy to replace the dead and rotting British Empire. Now, the Chinese Government, recognizing the likelihood of an imminent collapse of the trans-Atlantic financial system, has announced that the issue of a new financial architecture will be a core agenda item at the upcoming G-20 Summit in Hangzhou, China, September 4-5.

In recent discussions that Lyndon and Helga LaRouche have conducted with associates, Mrs. LaRouche has made it clear that, at the present moment, there is no sign from either the European Union or the United States

Xinhua

An illustration of China's Mars lander and rover released Aug. 23, 2016 by the Chinese State Administration of Science, Technology, and Industry for National Defense.

that they are willing to agree to the Chinese agenda of a new financial architecture. Hence, the question—now before the citizens of Europe and the United States—is whether they will show the same foresight and courage as the Germans of 1989 and seize upon this great moment to provide leadership.

G-20 and New Financial Architecture

According to an Aug. 15 press briefing from the Chinese Ministry of Foreign Affairs, President Xi Jinping intends to take personal leadership in guiding the upcoming G-20 Summit in Hangzhou, chairing over 10 different activities, and overseeing five of the key agenda topics, such as:

CCTV

Chinese Vice Minister of Finance Zhu Guangyao

• "enhancing policy coordination and breaking a new path for growth";
• "more effective and efficient global economic and financial governance";
• "robust international trade and investment";
• "inclusive and interconnected development";
• "other critical issues affecting the global economy."

Xi Jinping's intention is that the G-20 will "transform itself from a crisis response mechanism, into a long-acting governance mechanism." The title of the G-20 summit is "Toward an Innovative, Invigorated, Interconnected and Inclusive World Economy," which will undoubtedly send the British Monarchy into apoplectic fits, not to mention the fact that Russian President Vladimir Putin and Egyptian President Abdel Fattah el-Sisi will be the guests of honor.

As Helga Zepp-LaRouche emphasized, the very clear and singular purpose of this G-20 meeting is to force the new financial architecture on to the agenda. This was emphasized in the same Aug. 15 press briefing by Vice Minister of Finance Zhu Guangyao, who stated:

The G-20 Hangzhou Summit is of great significance for the strong, sustainable, and balanced growth of global economy. As the current world economy is complicated and changeable, the international community is paying high attention to the summit, and expects the summit to play a greater role in promoting global economic growth, safeguarding international financial stability, and dealing with risks and challenges. Since the beginning of this year, the financial channels of the G-20 have carried out cooperation and achieved positive progress in such areas as the global economic situation, the framework for strong, sustainable, and balanced growth, as well as investment and infrastructure, international financial architecture, and financial sector reform...

From the leadership of the nations representing the new paradigm, to the top criminals of Wall Street and the City of London, there is an almost universal recognition that the trans-Atlantic system is bankrupt. Even Lord Jacob Rothschild, in a publication for his investment house, admitted:

> ... the real ticking time bomb in this global Ponzi scheme is the immense market in financial derivatives...

The six months under review have seen central bankers continuing what is surely the greatest experiment in monetary policy in the history of the world. We are therefore in unchartered waters and it is impossible to predict the unintended consequences of very low interest rates, with some 30 percent vof global government debt at negative yields, combined with quantitative easing on a massive scale.

In a similar tone, *Wall Street on Parade* quotes analysts who describe the activity of the central banks as the largest Ponzi Scheme ever conceived. This was after the Swiss National Bank reported that it is holding $120 billion in stocks in its portfolio; it is only one of many central banks who can now print unlimited amounts of fresh money—money which carries the implicit backing of taxpayers—if stock investments (i.e., gambling bets) go bad and threaten the system. Meanwhile, the central banks are playing a pivotal role in driving stock markets up through the roof, increasing the disconnect of the financial markets from the real economy.

However, the real ticking time bomb in this global Ponzi scheme is the immense market in financial derivatives, as LaRouche has noted in his recent intervention around Deutsche Bank, an institution which has a derivatives portfolio the size of the *entire world GDP.*

As the leadership of China takes responsibility for putting the new financial architecture on the agenda for the G-20 Hangzhou Summit, they have simultaneously made a significant intervention into exposing this global derivatives crisis. According to hints in the *Wall Street Journal,* it was at the request of China that a recent report was issued by the Bank of International Settlements, which warns that there are no mechanisms in place at this time which can prevent a blow-out of the $600 trillion-plus, over-the-counter global financial derivatives bubble, should any one major party default on a derivatives contract.

Business Insider, in what can only be described as an almost painful understatement, was forced to admit that the results of that survey "are slightly terrifying," because if the derivatives clearing-houses fail to handle a crisis, then derivatives become "unexploded nuclear bombs nestling deep in the financial system." The *Wall Street Journal* further notes that China has placed the safety of central clearing houses "high on the agenda" of the upcoming G-20 summit.

As Helga Zepp-LaRouche has noted, there is presently nobody in the leadership of the European Union or the United States who intends to agree on the reality of this financial crisis, or on placing the urgent need for a new financial architecture on the agenda for the upcoming G-20 meeting. Think back to the G-7 summit earlier this year, when Japanese Prime Minister Shinzo Abe had said that the world economy faced the risk of another 2008 "Lehman shock" if appropriate action were not taken.

> ## Deutsche Bank's derivatives portfolio is as big as the entire world GDP.

However, due to the intervention of President Barack Obama and other stooges of the British Monarchy in the G-7 "leadership," a falsified rosy picture was presented instead.

In fact, according to *Bloomberg News,* Japan had intended to insert the danger of a collapse into the final communique. According to *Bloomberg,* a copy of the Japanese draft which it had obtained stated, "We recognize the risk of the global economy exceeding the normal economic cycle and falling into a crisis, if we did not take appropriate policy responses in a timely manner."

Furthermore, Abe insisted that the crisis could not be dealt with simply through monetary policy. At the T-20 Summit (Think-20) at the end of July, China's Vice Minister of Foreign Affairs Li Baodong made a similar point:

> Problems have not been solved, and new challenges are emerging. It's hard to boost the economy if you only rely on fiscal policy and monetary policy. You cannot ignore the impacts that the Brexit referendum, Turkey's political instability, and recent terrorism activities in France and Germany have had on the world economy.

Xinhua/Li Xueren

Chinese President Xi Jinping and his wife Peng Liyuan in a highly symbolic stroll on April 24, 2015 in Bandung, Indonesia, with African and Asian leaders as they commemorate the 60th anniversary of the historic 1955 Bandung Conference, which founded the Non-Aligned Movement.

Everyone has high expectations for the upcoming G-20 Summit in Hangzhou—we're all hoping that the G-20 can play a leading role, and direct a clear and bright path forward amidst the chaos of the international situation, and that it can reinvigorate the world's sluggish economy.

China, which hosted the T-20 event, made a very clear and unmistakable policy statement by inviting Helga Zepp-LaRouche and *EIR* Washington Bureau Chief Bill Jones, to attend that summit meeting. Mrs. LaRouche spoke on the first panel, and titled her remarks, "The New Silk Road Becomes the World Silk Road." In that panel, she pointedly described the early danger of a global financial collapse, and she counterposed to the unfolding crisis the need for a global Glass-Steagall policy, the principles of which would then become the start of any new financial architecture. She stated,

> *Wall Street Journal*: China has placed the safety of central clearing houses "high on the agenda" of the upcoming G-20 summit.

An uncontrolled collapse of the financial system of the trans-Atlantic sector would threaten to throw many parts of the world into chaos with unpredictable consequences. The so-called "tool-box" of financial instruments, which was decided upon after the 2008 crises instead of implementing true reforms, has been used up. The consequent "unorthodox monetary instruments," such as quantitative easing, negative interest rates, and helicopter money, have in large part produced the opposite of the intended effect.

The fact that the reintroduction of the FDR Glass-Steagall banking separation law has been adopted in the election platforms of both the Democratic and Republican parties in the United States, and the fact that there is a growing discussion in several European countries about reducing the future risk of the financial system by introducing Glass-Steagall criteria in Europe as well, create a very favorable precondition for agreeing upon a global Glass-Steagall Act at the upcoming G-20 summit.

What Mrs. LaRouche proposes is the crucial first step toward the beginning of a new financial architecture, without which the Global Silk Road is impossible—and vice versa. Their many-sided international diplomatic activity makes it clear that the leading nations of Russia, China and India know that it is time to act. Now we need the sane institutions within Europe,—especially within Germany as Lyndon LaRouche has identified,— and the institution of the Presidency within the United States, to act, and act fast.

Age of Destruction to Age of Reconstruction

The world is at a *punctum saliens,* and the discussion process within the various international forums during the month of September will be critical to determining which way it goes. Manhattan will be the central battle-ground for the question of the new financial architecture, as it is the home to both Wall Street and Alexander Hamilton, mortal foes since 1789. New York is also where the United Nations General Assembly will be held, starting on Sept. 13 and continuing until the end of the month, when heads of state will assemble to address each other, and the world.

However, much of what will be discussed there will be determined in the weeks before, at the various international forums that are also occurring in the month of September, starting with the Eastern Economic Forum in Vladivostok. Notably, Japanese Prime Minister Shinzo Abe and South Korean President Park Geun-hye will be in attendance there, in addition to President Xi Jinping and President Vladimir Putin.

At that Vladivostok forum, there will be a discussion of cooperation in large-scale infrastructure and other energy and resource investment opportunities, which will be an essential component to soothing tensions in an area manipulated by British geopolitics. The recent decision by Barack Obama to deploy the THAAD missile system into South Korea, has upset the strategic balance as part of Obama's war drive against the leading nations of Eurasia, Russia and China. Japan has historically been an asset of the British Monarchy and their geopolitical agenda, but with a series of recent moves by Abe, there appears to be the potential for Japan to shift toward cooperation with its Eurasian partners.

After the Eastern Economic Forum in Vladivostok, there is the ASEAN (Association of Southeast Asian Nations) summit, with participation of many other heads of state as well, which will convene amidst important ongoing dialogues between China and the Southeast Asian nations, especially as concerns the South China

Sea. All this will culminate with the crucial intervention made by the Chinese and their partners, to get the new financial architecture on the agenda at the G-20. The BRICS nations' heads of state will also meet on the sidelines of the G-20 summit. And from there, some heads of state will go to Manhattan, for the United Nations General Assembly which starts Sept. 13.

As the diplomatic staffs, foreign ministers, and some heads of state come to New York, they will arrive on the heels of an historic intervention by the members of the Schiller Institute and the Foundation for the Revival of Classical Culture, an intervention centered around performances of Mozart's *Requiem* and selected "Negro Spirituals" in honor of the victims of Sept. 11, both deceased and living, including those in other nations who have become the ongoing targets of the implications of 9/11. The horror of that day has not ended, since the wars that were launched based on the lies about who was responsible for 9/11 have not ended—from Afghanistan, to Iraq, to Libya and to Syria, with many other wars in between.

Last September, Vladimir Putin called for the creation of an international coalition to defeat terrorism, like the coalition which defeated the Nazis in World War II. That call was silently rejected by Barack Obama and others in the trans-Atlantic region who are under the control of the British Monarchy, those who instead would use terrorism for their geopolitical aims of breaking up the New Silk Road, led by China, Russia and India. Since last September, economic projects like the International North-South Transport Corridor have been initiated. Putin's brilliant diplomatic maneuvers have led to Turkey's joining the fight against terrorism in Syria. Egyptian President Al-Sisi has even hinted at a potential by Putin in negotiating a peace between Israel and Palestine.

Simultaneously, China has conducted crucial diplomatic work in the Middle East, illustrated by Xi Jinping's tour there earlier this year. India is also playing an important role, such as in Syria, where India's Deputy Foreign Minister Mubashir Javed Akbar recently met President Assad in Damascus, offering help to Syria. "The age of destruction should give way to the age of reconstruction," he said.

This age of reconstruction can only occur within the new financial architecture that China is fighting for. At present, there is no sign from the European Union or the United States that they will accept China's proposal,—which is why you, as a citizen, must act. History and walls are not moved by electoral politics and referendums; they are moved by ideas and by courage.

2016: America's Moment of Decision

by Diane Sare, LaRouche PAC Policy Committee

Were you there when they crucified my Lord?
Were you there when they crucified my Lord?
Oh, sometimes, it causes me to tremble, tremble,
  tremble—
Were you there when they crucified my Lord?
                                        —Traditional Spiritual

This is the fourth in a series of articles being presented by the LaRouche PAC National Policy Committee, in collaboration with Lyndon LaRouche, as part of his campaign to create a new Presidency over the coming 100 days.

Aug. 22—In November 2000, just days before the ill-fated U.S. Presidential Election (ill-fated because, like today, there was no possible "winning outcome"), Lyndon LaRouche wrote an extraordinary and prescient paper entitled, "Politics as Art," which concludes

> ...there is a precious lesson to be learned by all citizens and other residents of the United States, especially those oppressed by the ruinous policy-trends of the past thirty-five years, from, among relevant other sources, the polished form of what is called the Negro Spiritual.

Sixteen years later, I believe that this is more urgently true than at the time LaRouche wrote that earlier paper, which is why I have recently dedicated myself to the mission of engaging members of the Schiller Institute New York City Chorus in learning several African-American Spirituals as part of the upcoming 9-11 Memorial Series of performances of the Mozart Requiem.

Review what has happened since that dreadful November 2000 non-election and reflect on Mr. LaRouche's forecasts every step of the way. His forecast a

few days before the election was that no one would actually win. That seemed unimaginable at the time. How could you have a Presidential election in which there was no declared winner?

However, that was exactly what happened, and weeks of hanging chads later, George W. Bush was declared the winner. When "W" began searching for his Attorney General, and the name John Ashcroft was floated, Lyndon LaRouche warned, in a Jan. 3, 2001 international address, that this regime would only be able to govern through "Nazi tactics" and "crisis man-

White House Photo Office
Vice President Dick Cheney (left) and President George W. Bush.

agement" following a "Reichstag Fire event." Just nine months later, on Sept. 11, 2001, four planes were hijacked from the Newark (N.J.), Logan (Boston) and Dulles (Virginia) airports and flown into the World Trade Towers in Manhattan and the Pentagon, and one crashed in Shanksville, Penn. All the passengers and hijackers were incinerated. Thousands more were killed in the buildings which were struck.

Rather than launch a full investigation into the role of Saudi Arabia, which was home to 15 of the 19 hijack-

Left: The destroyed World Trade Center Towers after the 9/11/2001 attack.

wikimediacommons

U.S. Marines from the 2nd Battalion, 1st Marine Regiment, escort captured enemy prisoners of war in Iraq.

creative commons/BasicGov

Foreclosures devastated American communities. Millions were thrown out of their homes after the 2007-2008 banking crash.

ers, and into Saudi-British deals like the Prince Bandar/ Margaret Thatcher "Al-Yamamah" oil for weapons deal, which had created a giant slush fund capable of financing such an attack, Vice President Dick Cheney blocked all references to the Saudis, and instead sought to focus on Iraq. This included using disinformation extracted through torture to induce then-Defense Secretary Colin Powell to lie about an Iraq connection to Al-Qaeda in a subsequent speech given at the UN.

By March of 2003, with substantial prodding and complicity from the now-thoroughly-discredited and incriminated former British Prime Minister Tony Blair, a full invasion of Iraq was begun. On April 3, 2003, Lyndon LaRouche was interviewed on BBC about his opposition to the Iraq war and he identified explicitly the role of Vice President Dick Cheney, who moved after Sept. 11, 2001 to get his 1991 war plan back on track.

Also in 2003, on July 17, former UN weapons inspector Dr. David Kelly turned up dead after publicly accusing Tony Blair of "sexing up" (i.e. fabricating claims in) documents purporting to prove that Iraq possessed weapons of mass de-

LPAC

LaRouche PAC organizers' poster calling for a halt to foreclosures and for reorganizing the banking system under Glass-Steagall.

struction. Kelly's death was officially declared a suicide, but a team of medical doctors and others have subsequently expressed serious doubts that he could have died in the manner claimed by members of the Tony Blair Government. Their opinion is that he was most likely murdered.

As of June, 2016, nearly 4,500 Americans had been killed in Iraq. The suicide rate of Veterans in the United States is now over 8,000 per year. The suicide rates in the general population have increased significantly, as have rates of death by heroin overdose and alcoholism. This horrific increase in the death rates among Americans under the age of 55, at a time when they should be in the prime of life, is not a "natural" trend of human population growth. This increase in the death rate has occurred for two reasons. One, the satanically evil policies of the Bush and Obama Administrations, as both presidents have been tools of the British Monarchy, enforced by Wall Street and the FBI; and two, up until now, the American people have capitulated to Wall Street- and Hollywood-funded-and-orchestrated public opinion as it oozes out of their

Official White House Photo by Pete Souza

King Salman bids farewell to President Obama at his motorcade at Erga Palace.

"smart" phones through their wide-open eyes and ears to poison their minds.

Take the 2008 TARP. Remember that? In July of 2007, Lyndon LaRouche warned that the entire trans-Atlantic system was completely bankrupt and nothing could be done save it, and put forward the "Homeowners and Bank Protection Act" to halt foreclosures and reorganize the banking system under Glass-Steagall standards. Even though the truth came out that thousands of bankers and mortgage brokers had been engaged in outright theft and fraud, no major banker was jailed. Instead the very institutions and individuals who created the mess, received billions upon billions of dollars of bailouts and bonuses, creating unbearable inflationary expenses for the average American, as millions were expelled from their homes. Did Americans object?

No. They decided to go along with then-Treasury Secretary Hank Paulson (who has just endorsed Hillary Clinton for President) when he threatened the Congress that there would be troops in the streets if Wall Street didn't get this money, and the first $700 billion simply had to be issued, and then the next one and the next one...

The American people gave Cheney and Bush their permission to torture prisoners in their name at Abu Ghraib and elsewhere. They went along with Obama's bombing of Libya for 250 days, which the Congress never authorized; they accepted Susan Rice's lies about the " video" that caused the deaths of four American officials in Benghazi; and they went along with the ludicrous idea that we could have a health care system run by the IRS which would be "affordable." If it appeared on

Facebook that the far side of the moon might be made of green cheese, your neighbors would probably believe that as well. At least, in this case, the Chinese are actually going to investigate the truth of the matter, so interested Americans will have the benefit of knowing the truth.

If this were not absurdly tragic enough, now there is a new virtual reality fad, called "Pokemon Go," where supposedly adult humans are chasing non-existent creatures which pop up on their i-phones and GPS devices. These Pokemon players seem to be unable or unwilling to distinguish reality from fantasy. They seem to be so far gone, that Bertrand Russell is celebrating from the grave that it has now been determined how much it costs, per person, to make people believe, or at least profess to believe, "that snow is black." (Russell, *Impact of Science on Society*)

It was exactly this mini-Dark Age which LaRouche foresaw when he wrote in the aforementioned paper:

> Tomorrow, U.S. election-day, November 7, 2000, we shall witness an awful real-life tragedy on the world stage, the threat, if not yet the actuality of a new dark age. That threat is today's outgrowth of a long-standing, widespread violation of those Classical principles of statecraft which every citizen should have been given the right to know...

If the United States of America and Western Europe represented the planet as a whole, then the situation would be nearly hopeless. Happily, the United States is no longer the center of a unipolar world. There is a new leadership on the planet which represents about 70-plus nations and two thirds of the world's people. This leadership is embodied in Presidents Vladimir Putin of Russia and Xi Jinping of China.

Unlike the European Central Bank and the U.S. Federal Reserve with their helicopter money and negative interest rates, the Chinese have embarked on a program called "One Belt and One Road," which puts an end to geopolitics and "balance of power" infantilism, and replaces it with what President Xi calls "win-win cooperation." Over 25 years, 500 million Chinese people were lifted up out of poverty, and tens of millions are now learning to play musical instruments. China has just launched an ambitious program to attain levels of scientific literacy throughout the population as a whole. China is reaching out to nations in Africa and South America to help finance and build great projects,

Creative Commons/Moign Khawaja

Enlarging Gwadar deep-water port in Pakistan (seen here) is part of President Xi's blueprint for China's role in Eurasian economic development.

including ports, railroads and canals which will transform the global trade routes planet-wide.

Particularly since August of last year, when President Putin visited China for the spectacular V-J Day parade, these two heads of state have been running circles around the western leaders, including emphatically an increasingly desperate President Barack Obama, who, thanks to his own gigantic ego, still hasn't realized how badly he's been defeated.

It was Putin's announcement at last year's UN General Assembly that he was forming a coalition against terror, starting with defeating ISIS in Syria, which created the anvil, against which LaRouche organizers could hammer Obama's protection of the Saudi and British apparatus which ran the 9-11 attacks 15 years ago. Under these conditions, Obama could no longer avoid the release of the famous "28 pages" of the 9-11 Joint Congressional Inquiry which, despite lying U.S.-based media reports, are completely devastating to the Saudi Royal Family, as well as the FBI and CIA which covered up for them on behalf of the Bush Administration and the British Empire.

The actions of Xi Jinping and Putin have created the conditions for a radical change for the better within the United States, even though most Americans are oblivious to this potential. Partly, Americans are oblivious because of their own participation in the corruption of the nation. The corruption has found fertile ground in minds and souls which have been deprived of beauty.

As depraved as Americans have become, we are now presented with the opportunity to reverse the insanity of the last 50 years and chart a new course toward a bright future, thanks to the collaboration of Putin and Xi and the tireless commitment of Lyndon LaRouche over decades. With the release of the 28 pages, justice is near in the 9-11 case, and Glass-Steagall is a plank in both major party platforms. But to claim the victory, Americans have to remember what it is to be human—that is that human beings are *not* animals. That we are creative, and that that creativity is fueled by a love of our fellow man, and a love of mankind and posterity.

It was not the atrocity committed on Sept. 11, 2001 that nearly destroyed our Republic, but rather, it has been our own inaction in the face of a great evil which claimed the lives of thousands of our own citizens, not to mention millions of others,— which has almost rendered us unsalvageable.

This is why the African-American Spirituals, in their Classical form, as developed by the collaborators of Dvorak, are so important to our survival. Whenever she came to a choir rehearsal that I was directing, Sylvia

EIRNS/Alicia Cerritani

Rep. Walter Jones at a press conference to urge release of the 28 pages of the 9/11 report suppressed by Vice President Dick Cheney and President Obama. Joining him, left to right, members of the 9/11 families: Ellen Saracini; Terry, Justin, and Kaitlin Strada; and Abraham Scott.

Left to right: Bass-baritone William Warfield (1920-2002), baritone Dorceal Duckens, and longtime Lyndon LaRouche associate Dennis Speed, gathered around Sylvia Olden Lee (1917-2004) at a Schiller Institute conference in 2001.

Diane Sare, director of the Schiller Institute choruses in the New York City area, working with members of the Manhattan Schiller Institute Chorus.

Olden Lee used to say to the members of the chorus (in this case a largely African-American chorus in Washington, D.C.), "remember your Aunt Hattie." And she would clutch her hands together into her stomach and bow her head as if remembering some distant painful sacrifice, made by those who came before.

What she, Robert McFerrin, and Bill Warfield, all of whom I had the pleasure of observing both in performance and as teachers, conveyed very clearly, was that these songs are *not* slave songs. These are songs of noble human beings, unjustly held in bondage, who are expressing their dignity and their confidence in their own immortality. As Dr. Eugene T. Simpson, who was a trusted collaborator of Hall Johnson, writes in his book *The Hall Johnson Concert Spirituals*, "Perhaps the most important thing to remember in interpreting the spirituals is *that they are not songs of defeat, but songs of survival.*" I would go farther to say that they are songs of triumph of justice against evil, and of the victory of the human spirit.

As we organize the people of Manhattan and the surrounding areas to participate in the Schiller Institute Chorus, or to sign the LaRouche PAC petition to get justice for the victims of 9-11 by ensuring that such a thing never happens again, we are discovering a population that has not been able to reconcile their emotions about what occurred on that horrible day, and the fact that nothing has ever been done about it.

For example, those who lost a spouse say, "I just can't

bear to think about it any longer. I spent too many years obsessing about it. It ruined my life." Or, "My husband was a survivor, but all of his co-workers were killed. He was never the same, and our marriage ended as a result." Or a teacher who stated that she knew over 30 students in her school who had a parent who was killed. A police officer we met recently has just been diagnosed with a rare form of terminal cancer as a result of his work near Ground Zero. The list goes on and on. A handful of exceptional family members of the victims have had the fortitude to keep fighting for justice, even though to do so keeps the pain of loss very near the surface.

The African slaves and their descendants who created and sang the Spirituals under conditions of horrific physical deprivation, torture, and captivity succeeded in keeping their dignity and immortality as human beings with a direct relationship to God.

Mastery of these songs, in their polished form, as developed by Hall Johnson, H.T. Burleigh and others, is one pathway for Americans to access their own humanity. Once this spark has been reignited, as we saw in Selma, 1965, and Berlin, 1989, the people will no longer accommodate injustice. We are almost there.

Were you there when they rolled the stone away?
Were you there when they rolled the stone away?
Oh, sometimes, it causes me to tremble, tremble,
   tremble—
You were there when they rolled the stone away.
   —Spiritual as sung by Elvira Green

FROM MANHATTAN

The Truth which Redeems

by Dennis Speed

The man that hath no music in himself,
Nor is not moved with concord of sweet sounds,
Is fit for treasons, stratagems and spoils;
The motions of his spirit are dull as night
And his affections dark as Erebus:
Let no such man be trusted. Mark the music.
      —Shakespeare, *The Merchant of Venice*

The headline was surprising: "Extremist Pleads Guilty to Destroying Timbuktu Artifacts." The Aug. 22 *London Guardian* article written by Ruth Maclean reported: "The first defendant to plead guilty at the International Criminal Court has apologized to Mali and to mankind for destroying religious monuments in the ancient city of Timbuktu.

"Ahmad al-Mahdi admitted directing the destruction of nine mausoleums and a mosque door in 2012, when Timbuktu was controlled by rebels and members of al-Qaida in the Islamic Maghreb. At the opening of his trial for war crimes in The Hague, he expressed his 'deep regret' to the people of Timbuktu, to whom the monuments had been of great religious and cultural importance..."

This is a man that has forced himself to reverse his lethal, destructive axioms. This is the change in the American people, and humanity, that Abraham Lincoln sought and demanded in his Second Inaugural Address. This man's reversal shows the humanity that can be

Twitter/ICC-CPI

Ahmad al-Faqi al-Mahdi admitted guilt to the International Criminal Court in The Hague for destroying historical and religious monuments of great cultural and religious importance in Timbuktu, Mali in 2012, expressing deep regret for his actions.

evoked, elicited, even in the darkest of situations, from the seemingly worst of human beings, if the weapons of poetry are understood and deployed. This is what was recently achieved in Palmyra, Syria, in the Classical music concert presented by Russia in a re-consecration of that city's temples, libraries and monuments—"bare, ruined choirs where late the sweet birds sang"—with the solo violin playing of the *Chaconne* written by Johann Sebastian Bach.

The city of Timbuktu, located in Mali, Africa, was a terminus of the Silk Road. In the Fourteenth Century, it was the second largest court in the world, one of the great centers of learning, and legendary for its wealth. Today, it has been sacked, and many of its privately held and protected libraries destroyed, a casualty, not merely of the al-Ghazali tradition of "The Destruction of Philosophy," but of a cultural warfare policy, seen also in 2003 with the sacking of Iraq's Baghdad Museum, and seen, yet again, in the destruction of Syria's cultural artifacts today by forces largely created and supported by the "barbarians at the gate" of civilization from the Obama Administration: Susan Rice, Victoria Nuland, Samantha Power, and others. These catastrophes mark the final, though not triumphant, phase of British dominance of American foreign policy by the British-inspired, Paris-centered and American-staffed Congress for Cultural Freedom launched in the late 1940s.

Onslaught Against the Human Identity

Seven decades ago, the British Intelligence/State Department organization known as the *Congress for Cultural Freedom* (CCF) launched a campaign of cultural war on the nations of the trans-Atlantic. Their foci were France, Germany, and the United States, with particular emphasis on breaking the connection of Americans to "German" Classical music—that is, the tradition of Mozart, Beethoven, Brahms, and Bach's influence in America. Conductor Wilhelm Furtwängler was the main recipient of their opprobrium, and a not-so-subtle equation of "Classical" with "Nazi" was popularized, expressed by the virtual-reality term, "the authoritarian personality."

The alternative "personality" to the "authoritarian type" could be produced, the CCF claimed, through "cultural freedom of expression." Suddenly, and for the first time, jazz musicians found themselves traveling on behalf of the State Department to promote America's "cultural freedom of expression"—although they themselves were prohibited in their own country from sleeping in the same hotels or eating in the same restaurants with (or even by) their Washington, D.C. State Department sponsors. American Abstract Expressionist painter Jackson Pollock's entire career, and the careers of scores of other "artists," were made by the CCF. This, combined with the Princeton Radio Research Project's 1950s-60s "war on American ear-drums" called AM "Top 40" radio, was part of the CCF's decades-long bombardment of several successive generations of Americans with unrelenting ugliness in the museums, concert halls, and parks of the nation.

The Congress for Cultural Freedom's *Paris Review* was founded in 1953 by CIA agent Peter Matthiesson, but actually as a British "franchise" intelligence outfit, staffed by several Anglophiles, particularly John Train, Prince Sadruddin Aga Khan, and others. Such creatures are the secret to the destruction of three generations of American culture, through bad music, bad painting, and atrocious poetry; herein lies the connection to the recent events in Timbuktu, and between what people have been miseducated to believe are the unrelated fields of literature, espionage, terror-

ism and cultural warfare. For purposes of brevity and direct relationship to Lyndon LaRouche's Manhattan Project, we will focus on the figure of Wall Street financial spook, "literary figure," and all-around stinker, John Train.

Train, an investment banker on Wall Street since 1958 (Smith, Train Counsel) was an early managing

cc/Melissa Eagan, WNYC New York Public Radio

CIA agent Peter Matthiessen, founder CCF's Paris Review.

John Train

cc/ErlingMandelmann.ch

Prince Sadruddin Aga Khan

Nancy Wong

George Plimpton

editor of the *Paris Review.* He did post-graduate work at the Sorbonne, where he founded, with others, the *Review* in 1953. Born in 1928, Train attended Harvard and roomed at Eliot House there with Prince Aga Khan and George Plimpton, later the publisher, and chief editor, respectively, of the magazine. (Aga Khan and Plimpton were both editors of the *Harvard Lampoon.*) Peter Matthiessen was recruited to the CIA at Yale, and in turn recruited Plimpton as the chief editor. Prince Aga Khan's money, and foundation, were used as a

EIRNS/Stuart Lewis

Dennis King, left, Chip Berlet, right.

EIRNS

Lyndon LaRouche advocating what later became the SDI.

EIRNS/Stuart Lewis

Michael Hudson, left, and Bryan Chitwood, right.

cover for CIA financing of the project.

Get LaRouche

Decades later, but before John Train would deploy his "literary connections" to form and direct the "Get LaRouche Task Force" in April of 1983, he would found the *Afghan Relief Committee* (ARC), in his Wall Street offices. This was the major financial conduit for the mujahideen in America, the operation which was the same that was recruiting Bush family friend Salem bin Laden's half-brother, Osama bin Laden, as a contract operative for the "Islamic Fundamentalist Card" war begun by Zbigniew Brzezinski in Afghanistan in the summer of 1979. Train created the ARC in 1980. (Tens of millions may have flowed through the ARC conduit's auspices, including money from Saudi Arabia now fully documented in the recently released 28 pages of the 2002 Joint Congressional Inquiry Report on 9/11.) Then, in 1983,— one month after President Ronald Reagan stunned the world, including the Anglo-

American establishment, with his March 23 announcement of the LaRouche-designed Strategic Defense Initiative (SDI) policy that would have ended the world's present thermonuclear chicken-game,— Train was tasked with the destruction of the SDI policy, by character-assassinating and destroying Lyndon LaRouche.

Having spent decades obliterating the minds of American and European students with his *Paris Review,* Train knew how to assemble the appropriate scribblers for this task. They included Sol Sanders, former editor of *Business Week;* Virginia Armat, former editor of *Reader's Digest* and personal editor to Train; John Rees, publisher of *Information Digest;* scribblers Michael Hudson, Chip Berlet and Dennis King; the late financier Richard Mellon Scaife, and many others. The effect of Train's efforts, combined with those of the Justice Department and leading assets of British intelligence, was that LaRouche was eventually successfully prosecuted and railroaded in Virginia's "rocket docket," and sent to prison on Jan. 27, 1989. The SDI policy, rejected by Russia's Yuri Andropov in 1983, a rejection "seconded" by the incarceration of LaRouche, would never be implemented.

The cost of the LaRouche incarceration for the American people was far greater than the cost to LaRouche himself, or to his organization. The American Presidency never had its greatest representative since Franklin Roosevelt and John Kennedy ascend to that office. The country forfeited its future for forty years. Two generations were destroyed through the post-rock/drug/sex counterculture. America descended into becoming the greatest debtor nation in history. It became boorish, venal, and stupid. And none of this was necessary. It was the product of smallness, of practicality. And it was the reason that the mass murder of September 11, 2001, could occur in the way that it did, and could go unpunished in the way that it has.

The present collapse of American culture—drug overdoses, rampant illiteracy, unemployability for productive work, teenage suicides—is the true legacy of the Congress for Cultural Freedom's war against LaRouche, as an "authoritarian personality," as that war was waged against Furtwängler, and in a different way against Albert Einstein. Ugliness, however, has never been as powerful as beauty, in any area of human thought. Lyndon LaRouche and his movement have re-emerged again, particularly in Manhattan, and this by using the power of what LaRouche once referred to as "Politics as Art."

Manhattan—Overcoming Tragedy

In an exchange at the Saturday, Aug. 20, LaRouche Manhattan dialogue, the following report on New York organizing was given:

In the process leading up to the concerts in the Bronx, we have been getting a response which gives an indication of the political effect of our music work. In the Italian neighborhood, we've been getting an opening from people who are interested in studying up on our Classical culture atmosphere—people who a long time ago, actually had Caruso sing in their back room.

The Spanish communities have been inviting us to their carnivals to announce our concerts. The Muslim community has committed themselves to bringing their youth. And we found out that different community leaders, when we came to them to tell them about the concert, already knew about it or were committed to coming.

Furthermore, we have been going to offices of different politicians in the area, with "singing telegrams," singing the "Alleluia, viva la musica" canon, inviting these politicians to our concerts, and asking them to circulate the concert invitations, which has inspired them to promote our concerts and participate. We have even been invited to sing at an event.

The general response is that people see,— they look at the situation with the street violence and the terrorism, and they acknowledge that the situation is desperate. And then when we come and present the idea of freedom through beauty, they respond very immediately.

So my question is what do you think we will be able to harvest out of this process?

A participant in the dialogue answered:

When you began talking, I was just reminded of something that once happened. I was once in a conversation with Mr. LaRouche, and we were talking about François Rabelais; and for people who know the books *Gargantua and Pantagruel,* they appear to be these very extended episodes which are very funny, and they seem to be very wild and obscene, and at the same time very insightful. And what he said to me was: "Well, you have to understand that this is a book about tragedy. That people,— that era of France with Rabelais, we're talking about the early 16th Century,— was tragic. It was a society which was dead-ending. And what he was doing was inventing a language, a capability, something like what Boccaccio and Petrarca did with Italian, and in a different way what Chaucer, and then later Shakespeare, did with English,— a way to allow people to remove themselves from a state of tragedy."

The United States is in a tragic circumstance which a lot of people believe to be predestined effectively now, or inevitable,— it's so closed you can't do anything about it. The music gives people courage. It connects them to something deeper in their own nature, in which they resonate, because you are allowing them to find a way to place their own voice,— you know the voice of their true selves. Now, this comes from some work that was done—John's here and some others—who 30 years ago, did some work with

LaRouche on a *Manual on Tuning and Registration,* in which the contention was that the performance of Classical music, and the access to Classical culture, had been completely destroyed, or at least had been distorted, because of the arbitrary raising of the pitch and the distortion of the effect and the unity of effect of Classical music.

And this is an *essential* political war, and what we're doing in our performances of the *Requiem,* and the process,

RT/livestream coverage

After the liberation of this nearly 2000-year-old amphitheater in Palmyra, Syria, in which ISIS had executed dozens of people, distinguished Russian conductor Valery Gergiev conducted a living memorial on behalf of the living, using classical music to remoralize people and introduce a new politics.

the choral process leading up to it, which is even more important, because people are actually involved in participating in trying to sing it and now,— now organizing for it, what that does, is it returns people's voice. Because they know— they can hear the braying and the gnawing and the gnashing of teeth that you get with a Trump or a Hillary or all this other stuff. People are aware of that ... but they don't have a voice!

So, the Manhattan Project is dedicated to this. And we have a few people here, who because of their work for decades, have a capability that doesn't exist anywhere, actually, maybe in the world,— certainly not in the United States. So I think what's going to come out of this, is that you're going to have hundreds of people who will have gone through the process, thousands of people who will hear the performances, and some scores of people, young people in particular, who are going to want to do the same thing. And if you can get *that,* then you can get the basis to create genius.

Mozart, in particular, in this case, is excellent for this, and John or others may want to say something about it. And the *Requiem* is going to cause people to remember the crime of 9/11, but in a way which is elevated; they're elevated above it. They don't have to be drowned in despair by thinking about it. I think,— we were told by one of our organizers in California, a violinist,

that she's coming to the performance; but she's bringing with her the badge and the shield of a firefighter from California, and she will be wearing this during the performance. He can't be here, but he wants his badge and his shield here, and he wants that given to the Brooklyn fire department, in particular, which lost 23 firefighters.

But the concept is, that this is a Living Memorial, and that the people who are performing are performing not on behalf of the dead—no. They're performing on behalf of this newly found voice of the American people. That's what we're trying to do. We're introducing a new politics, a new political practice into America; it's one that Lyn [LaRouche] has always insisted on but we now know how to do it. And I think that's what's going to come out of this. I think we're going to find that manifest in hundreds, if not thousands of people joining our movement from this standpoint. And that's the beginning of the basis of a cultural Renaissance.

The Solution: a Human Culture

What Lyndon LaRouche often refers to as voice placement—the statement of an urgent great idea, properly vocalized and written, beautifully composed, and designed to increase the capacity of people for "profound and impassioned conceptions respecting man and nature," is absent in today's America, and must be supplied by a new movement. That new movement is what LaRouche refers to as the New Presidency. John Sigerson,— the director of the chorus that will present four performances of the Mozart *Requiem* as a "Living Memorial" to the 3,000 Americans and others murdered in the still-unsolved crime of Sept. 11, 2001,— recently recounted his experiences at a four-day discussion and workshop process in nearby upstate New York. Sigerson was able to engage with more than a dozen of the best new Classical singers and musicians in the New York area (and several from around the world) in hours of work, using the proper tuning pitch of C=256 cycles per second. An entire facility in the area has now re-tuned its pianos to accommodate this needed change. Discussions were wide-ranging, far beyond the technicalities of musical performance and interpretation.

In addition, as he and Diane Sare, founder of the Schiller Institute New York City Community Chorus, prepare the non-professional volunteer chorus for the extraordinary set of performances to occur now in less than a month, something else has begun, spontaneously, to occur. The discussion process around Mozart's *Requiem* has prompted, increasingly, involuntary comparison to the present electoral and national situation. It would be nearly impossible for this not to occur. But why is Mozart's *Requiem* essential to be presented at this point?

The horror and ugliness of the Presidential Administrations of the past fifteen years demand a requiem, not for the dead—and not for the living dead—but for the conditions which perpetuate that feeling of desperation now epidemic in every part of our nation. A New Presidency begins with a properly placed intoning of Mozart's *Requiem* as a key to help unlock the doorway into a new future for all mankind, already offered, but still unseen and unacknowledged in this country.

Through the work of Lyndon and Helga LaRouche, and the efforts of the leadership of Russia, China, and the nations allied with them, the possibility now exists of a new world based on the scientific optimism of the unlimited potential of the human mind. The LaRouche PAC Manhattan Project, and the choral process that it expresses, is building the new assembly by which that future, and its New Presidency, can be brought into being—by the "sweet power of song," possessed only by those who, whatever crimes they may have committed or tolerated in the past, now have the courage to reverse their axioms and those of the dying cultures that oppress them.

II. Something New Under the Sun

Now There are No Precedents

Aug. 18—The present period in history is totally new in its characteristics; it is not comparable with anything in past human history. For such reasons, only a very few individuals have been able to generate in their own minds, the conception of what the characteristics are of this unprecedented epoch: individuals such as Albert Einstein, Krafft Ehricke, and Lyndon and Helga LaRouche. Because it resembles nothing in their experience, and nothing they have heard or read about, the great majority of mere mortals have no criteria with which to judge or understand it; they are totally at sea. It is for this reason that groups which are as small in number as Lyndon LaRouche's Manhattan Project, can become decisive in determining influences, precisely at this moment. They alone can see their way forward, even if sometimes dimly or gropingly. The rest are totally blind, or, as Helga Zepp-LaRouche often says, completely "clueless."

In 2018, a Chinese mission will reach the far side of the Moon,— provided that we succeed in defeating the British Empire's forces of chaos before then. This will be part of an entire broad program of discovering and exploring the unrealized implications of Einstein's fundamental discoveries, as Lyndon LaRouche has pointed out. And, as space genius Krafft Ehricke forecast,— with LaRouche,— the energy flux density at the disposal of mankind will lead up to fusion power, from there to matter-antimatter reactions, and from there to levels which cannot even be named today.

Provided we overcome the present obstacles represented by Obama and the British Empire, we are moving into what Helga Zepp-LaRouche has called "a new era where we become truly human."

Similarly, what one might have called the "system of alliances," which is now spanning and criss-crossing Eurasia, and spreading out from there, is not actually a "system of alliances" at all, in any sense of those words known from the past. Rather, it is in reality a projection backwards into the present, from the future universe which incorporates the future discoveries brought back from the far side of the Moon. Putin, along with China,

has incorporated the principles of the Peace of Westphalia, but they have gone far, far beyond anything like it. Just start with the extraordinary relationship which has been achieved between Russia and China. Don't you realize that these are nations which fought a seven-month undeclared war on the Ussuri River as recently as 1969? Now, not only do they have regular summits between the Presidents and regular summits between the Prime Ministers; that's the least of it. There are no fewer than thirteen intergovernmental commissions which are in continual contact all the time. All the many differences and disagreements,— and there are many,— are continually being worked out throughout all the breadth and depth of both governments.

"And we always find solutions," Putin added in describing this.

The process of achievement of this extraordinary relationship has been a subject of in-depth study by China's Dr. Ren Lin, who spoke at the Schiller Institute Berlin Conference in June, and by many other Chinese and Russian scholars.

This unprecedented achievement is at the heart of the BRICS process, and the development of the New Silk Road. It was the heart of the Russia-India-China Strategic Triangle concept of Putin's predecessor, the late former Russian Prime Minister Yevgeny Primakov. The genesis goes back, not only to Lyndon and Helga LaRouche's concept of the Productive Triangle and the Eurasian Land-Bridge, but back earlier to LaRouche's Strategic Defense Initiative, which had a formative impact on Russia, even though Russia's once leader Yury Andropov had rejected it on behalf of his British masters.

This new system, nation-state relations of the future, beyond the nation-state, as LaRouche has long forecast, is striding rapidly over the entirety of the Eurasian continent and more broadly, as we approach the Vladivostok Eastern Economic Forum of Sept. 2-3, the G-20 meeting in Hangzhou, China, Sept. 4-5, the United Nations General Assembly opening on Sept. 13, and the BRICS Summit in Goa, India, Oct. 15-16.

Putin's Eurasian Alliance

by Dean Andromidas

Aug. 21—In a discussion of the recent sudden, dramatic rapprochement between Russia and Turkey, Lyndon LaRouche maintains that this represents Turkey's joining the alliance of Eurasian nations created under the leadership of Russian President Vladimir Putin, and goes well beyond simply the improvement of bilateral relations. President Putin's strategy dovetails with China's "One Belt One Road," New Silk Road policy. Putin has created a new reality across Eurasia, a reality the Europeans are failing to recognize, but which cannot be reversed.

The meeting between Russian President Putin and his Turkish counterpart Recep Tayyip Erdogan on Aug. 9 in St. Petersburg, marked Turkey's joining this new reality. The meeting laid to rest the eight-month crisis caused by Turkey's shooting down of a Russian warplane operating over Syria, and put bilateral relations well on the road to deepening economic, political, and strategic cooperation.

Erdogan described that meeting as a "milestone," and told reporters afterwards that the two leaders were committed to increasing trade and tourism, and had prioritized the Turkish Stream Gas Pipeline and the Akkuyu nuclear power station. He added that they had discussed using their own currencies for bilateral trade. Erdogan was accompanied by a large economic and business delegation which held a meeting parallel to the summit.

The two presidents agreed that a High Level Strategic Council (HLSC) of their two countries would meet

kremlin.ru

Turkish President Recep Tayyip Erdogan (left) and Russian President Vladimir Putin at their Aug. 9 summit at St. Petersburg.

in December in St. Petersburg. They also committed themselves to expand cooperation in the defense-industry sector.

On the crucial question of ending the Syria war, they created a tripartite mechanism of high-level representatives of each country's intelligence agency, foreign ministry, and defense ministry, which held its first meeting on Aug. 11. They also established a hotline between the Chiefs of Staff of their respective armed forces.

The Putin-Erdogan Summit occurred within 24 hours of the historic Aug. 8 summit among President Putin; the President of Iran, Hassan Rouhani; and the President of Azerbaijan, Ilham Aliyev, whose discussions centered on the urgency of making the International North-South Transport Corridor operational, which will create a rail link from Iran's Persian Gulf port at Bandar Abbas to Europe, through Russia and

Russian President Putin, Iran President Hassan Rouhani, and Azerbaijan President Ilham Aliyev meeting at the historic Aug. 8 trilateral summit in Baku, Azerbaijan.

Azerbaijan. This will facilitate the ability of South Asian countries—India, in particular—and the Southeast Asian nations, to skirt the Suez Canal and send their cargoes more directly by sea and rail to Central Asia, Russia, and Europe. This route will reduce transportation time by almost one-third.

Following the three Presidents' summit, the three foreign ministers, Azerbaijan's Elma Mammadyarov, Iran's Mohammed Javad Zarif, and Russia's Sergey Lavrov, held a joint press conference where Mammadyarov made the point that Azerbaijan's unresolved Nagorno-Karabakh conflict with Armenia impedes the development of the North South Corridor. But now, "opportunities were created for the settlement of [the] Nagorno-Karabakh conflict after the meeting of Presidents in St. Petersburg," he said.

As a result of the Russo-Turkish Summit, Turkey will be able to help play a role in resolving the Nagorno-Karabakh conflict. Turkey historically has had poor relations with Armenia, and has backed Azerbaijan in the Nagorno-Karabakh conflict, but now Turkey will be sitting at the same table to help resolve it. For Turkey, the resolving of this conflict would open the East-West rail link to Turkey and the Black Sea, which would in-

tersect the North South Corridor via Armenia,— whose rail links to Turkey and Azerbaijan have been cut because of this conflict.

In further diplomatic steps to begin implementing this Eurasian alliance, the foreign ministers of Iran and Turkey have exchanged visits to Ankara and Tehran respectively, where both the Syrian and the Nagorno-Karabakh issues were raised, and the groundwork for a future summit of the Presidents of Turkey, Iran, and Azerbaijan was laid.

Kazakstan, one of the most important countries in Central Asia and a member of the Eurasian Economic Union (along with Russia, Armenia, Kyrgyzstan and Belarus), is also playing a major role in this Eurasian alliance. Kazakstan President Nasultan Nazarbayev was a key actor in mediating the Russo-Turkish rapprochement. He became the first head of state to visit Turkey after the coup-attempt, during which he discussed the possibility of Turkey joining the Eurasian Economic Union.

Thus a process has moved forward that opens the promise to create an arc of peace and development from Syria and Turkey, deep into Central Asia and on into China.

INTERVIEW

Iran Will Contribute to the International Thermonuclear Fusion Experiment

by Marsha Freeman

Editorial Note: The following interview with Dr. Mahmood Ghoranneviss is printed here, not only due to the importance of what Dr. Ghoranneviss reports, as pregnant with potential as that report is, but also for the reader to perceive the significance of Iran's entry into a leading role for fusion energy research, within the greater context of the history-changing developments which are now taking hold within the entirety of Southwest Asia and the extended region of the "Middle East" in general.

Beginning with the Aug. 8 summit meeting of Russian President Vladimir Putin, the President of Iran, Hassan Rouhani, and the President of Azerbaijan, Ilham Aliyev, and continuing with the meeting between Russian President Putin and Turkish President Recep Tayyip Erdogan on Aug. 9 in St. Petersburg, a change in the entire course of human history and a pathway out of the current global crisis has now been opened up. An effective strategy against terrorism, an attainable perspective for peace, and rapidly expanding potentials for economic development are now all achievable goals. The Putin-Rouhani discussions concerning the development of the North-South Transport Corridor, together with the ever-more determined efforts by the Chinese government to extend a policy of economic development through its "One Belt One Road" initiative, have now made clear how close a new global human potential is to fruition.

It is precisely this perspective for global economic development which Lyndon LaRouche has championed since 1975, and it is the proposal for Eurasian economic development which he presented at a seminar in Washington, D.C. in 1997.

It is within that context that EIR is most grateful and happy to present the following interview, which among other things, demonstrates Iran's determination to play a leading role in the new Scientific Renaissance.

—the Editors of EIR

Interview with Dr. Mahmood Ghoranneviss

"Politicians have programs just for less than four years, but great people have programs for their grandchildren."

—Dr. Mahmood Ghoranneviss

Last year's nuclear agreement between Iran and the P5+1 nations of China, France, Germany, Russia, the United Kingdom, and the United States, created the possibility for Iran to participate in the world's leading fusion experiment, the International Thermonuclear Experimental Reactor, (ITER), which is under construction in France. Iran is well placed to contribute to this worldwide research project, as it has had an active program

Dr. Ghoranneviss, Dean of the Plasma Physics Research Center of the Science & Research Branch of the Islamic Azad University in Iran.

in fusion research since 1975, and in 1994, established the Plasma Physics Research Center of the Science & Research Branch of the Islamic Azad University, northwest of Tehran. Dr. Mahmood Ghoranneviss is the founder, and current Dean, of the Center. He is also now Iran's official representative to ITER.

In an interview published in the Sept. 18, 2015 issue of *EIR*, Dr. Ghoranneviss described the fusion research activities underway in Iran, and provided photographs of Iran's IR-T1 tokamak. He expressed the expectation on the part of Iran's fusion scientists that Iran could make significant contributions to the global fusion

Plasma Physics Research Center/Islamic Azad University

Iran's IR-T1 tokamak, shown here in 1985, contributes to global fusion research under the small tokamaks program of the International Atomic Energy Agency.

effort. Through a series of recent meetings and discussions, Iran's role in ITER is being defined, and activities are underway to bring Iran into the mainstream of international fusion research. On Aug. 16, Dr. Ghoranneviss provided answers to questions concerning these recent developments, posed to him by *EIR* Technology Editor Marsha Freeman.

EIR: When did the discussions begin on Iran's collaboration on ITER?

Ghoranneviss: As you know, in the P5+1 agreement, one of the points is that Iran can participate in the ITER project. For the past four years, the Plasma Physics Research Center (PPRC) has already been on the list of countries that are active in fusion research, and Iran's PPRC has one of the active tokamaks in the Middle East. There are two tokamaks in Pakistan, and one in Egypt.

On Aug. 28, 2015, just one month after the nuclear agreement was signed, the Director-General of ITER, Dr. Bernard Bigot, suggested collaboration between the PPRC and ITER. I accepted his suggestion, and the necessary steps were taken toward this collaboration. Dr. Bigot said that for full cooperation in this project, we would ultimately need the agreement of the ITER members (Europe, Russia, the USA, China, South Korea, Japan, and India). Hopefully, in the future, the above countries will accept Iran as a participant in the ITER project as one of the main members. It is also possible to be an associate member of ITER.

Dr. Bigot asked me to get formal approval for cooperation from Iran's government. Iran has a long history of research in fusion, and because fusion nuclear energy is a clean energy source, Iran's government was interested in joining ITER. Therefore, as a consultant to Dr. Sorena Sattari, who is the Iranian Vice-President for Science and Technology, I discussed this matter with him. He proposed to get the government's approval, and fortunately he succeeded in two days. We then sent the formal acceptance letter to join the ITER project to Dr. Bigot. I was selected as Iran's representative for the ITER project by Dr. Sattari and Dr. Ali Akbar Salehi, the head of the Atomic Energy Organization of Iran.

EIR: When was the first formal meeting of scientists from Iran with ITER representatives?

Ghoranneviss: Our first meeting was in Vienna, in February 2016. In this meeting, I presented Iran's fusion research activities and Dr. Bigot presented the ITER project's activities. There were five people at the meeting from Iran and four people from the ITER project, and one person from the International Atomic Energy Agency, which is headquartered in Vienna.

EIR: What were the options for Iran that were presented by Dr. Bigot at that meeting?

Ghoranneviss: Dr. Bigot discussed the membership conditions and suggested that Iran can be either an associate member or a main member of ITER. He mentioned, however, that 40% of the project is already done, and major components, such as superconductors and other parts, have already been built by the seven partner countries and have been transferred to France. Each member has expended 1.2 billion euros for its contribution to building ITER. Therefore, if we were to become a main member, we would have to pay the same amount over 10 years.

EIR: What are the requirements that Iran would have to meet to become an associate member?

Ghoranneviss: To become an associate member,

ITER

The Iranian delegation visiting ITER on July 1. From left: Dr. Bernard Bigot, Director-General of ITER; Dr. Ali Akbar Salehi, head of the Atomic Energy Organization of Iran; Dr. Sorena Sattari, Iranian Vice President for Science and Technology; Dr. Ghoranneviss.

one requirement is to educate Masters and PhD students in the nuclear fusion research field in Iran, and later to join one of the more developed and active tokamaks, such as France's Tore Supra superconducting tokamak experiment, which has been upgraded and is now known as WEST. Later, we could join the ITER project. Since the PPRC has been working on diagnostic instruments for its own tokamak, creating their design and construction, ITER presented us with a list of diagnostics, from which to choose for development for ITER. We have chosen some to develop, from those that were suggested to us.

EIR: What meeting followed that first one in Vienna?

Ghoranneviss: At our next meeting, which was held in France, Dr. Sattari and Dr. Salehi and I attended, with some other scientists from Iran. We visited the French Atomic Energy Commission, CEA, and the details of Tore Supra activities were discussed. It was decided to first build a small superconducting tokamak in Iran, with the help of world scientists, along with the ITER project. Then, after the design and construction of diagnostics to make plasma measurements, and after all the parts had been checked, they would be transferred to the ITER project.

The second part of our meeting in France was held in Cadarache at the ITER site. Dr. Salehi suggested that it would be better for Iran to become an associate member of ITER for two years, and later join the project as an 8th full member. This suggestion was accepted by Dr. Bigot and his colleagues. Now, I am gathering both theoretical and experimental experts to develop the diagnostics.

EIR: Has there been follow-up from your visit to France?

Ghoranneviss: After coming back from France in late June, Dr. Salehi invited four scientists from the Atomic Energy Commission of France to visit the PPRC, the Atomic Energy Organization of Iran, and some state universities. The French scientists presented reports on their research activities at the meeting. We expect to sign a contract with CEA France and the ITER project soon.

By the way, the Iran superconducting tokamak (Iran-SC-Tokamak) must be a high-tech tokamak, for operation in 2025-2027. It must develop additional innovations to help ITER and the planning of the post-ITER next-step fusion demonstration reactor, DEMO. Iran is making a huge investment in fusion experiments and also in human resources. So, the international community should participate in this investment for a common purpose, which is DEMO!

EIR: So the plan is to proceed in the near term with the very advanced superconducting tokamak, as an associate member of ITER, and consider full membership later on?

Ghoranneviss: If the goal of Iran is to construct a superconducting tokamak, which will be similar to, but a bit more advanced with respect to South Korea's KSTAR or Europe's WEST experiment, by that time, ITER members will invite Iran to become a main member with honor. To accomplish this requires great determination and needs a serious commitment by Iran for this long-term program. Now is the time for Iran to increase the quality, not the quantity of its fusion research!

EIR: What is the next step?

Ghoranneviss: First, we must prepare a meeting in Tehran and invite the experts and scientists from ITER member countries and others to several forums. Of course, we must also create an Iranian domestic agency to directly interface with the ITER organization.

And then, we need to establish an international scientific committee to determine the critical issues for ITER/DEMO in order to plan for the construction of the new Iranian tokamak with new innovations, not only for Iran, but also for all international users. I believe that Iran must receive about 30% of the costs of the Iran-SC-Tokamak from the international community. This is just my opinion.

Developing fusion energy is a long-term program. The politicians have programs just for less than four years, but the great people have programs for their grandchildren.

ITER

The first major components for ITER began arriving on the construction site in December 2015. It will be, by far, the largest tokamak in the world, designed to produce 500 MW of fusion energy.

Diagnostics

This is the list of diagnostics suggested to Iran for design and fabrication by Prof. Michael Walsh, the head of diagnostics in ITER.

The diagnostics could be broken down into 8 groups:

1. **Magnetics**
   - Continuous external Rogowski
   - Out vessel discrete Coils
   - Out Vessel Steady state Sensors
   - Partial and continuous flux loops
   - Halo Rogowski Coils
   - In-vessel coils
2. **Neutrons**
   - Radial neutron camera
   - Vertical neutron camera
   - Microfission chambers
   - Neutron flux monitoring (ex-vessel)
   - Gamma ray spectrometers
   - High resolution neutron spectrometer
3. **Optical**
   - Thomson scattering
   - Interferometer
   - Polarimeter
4. **Bolometric**
   - Bolometers
5. **Microwave**
   - Reflectometer
   - Interferometer
6. **Spectroscopic**
   - CXRS
   - Hα spectroscopy
   - VUV plasma
   - X ray crystal spectrometer Soft X ray radial spectrometer
   - H phase hard X ray monitor
   - Beam emission spectrometer
   - Divertor VUV spectroscopy
   - VUV edge imaging
   - XCRS edge imaging
   - Visible/IR cameras
7. **Neutral particle analyzer**
   - Neutral particle analyzer
8. **Plasma facing and operational**
   - Thermocouples
   - Pressure gauges
   - Residual gas analyzers
   - IR thermography
   - Langmuir probes
   - Erosion monitor
   - Dust monitor
   - Tritium monitor

Every Day Counts In Today's Showdown To Save Civilization

III. Save Deutsche Bank

THE GERMAN QUESTION

The Spark for the Collapse, or a Driver for World Development

Aug. 20—If Deutsche Bank is allowed to descend into an uncontrolled collapse, exploding the largest pool of derivatives among the world's banks, not only will the German economy be destroyed, but all of Europe and the United States with it. And yet, that is what is on the agenda, literally any day. Yet another voice from the financial elite screamed the alarm Aug. 16: "Deutsche is in more trouble than people realize," said Brad Lamensdorf of Ranger Equity Bear in an interview with *The Express* of London. "Something is very, very broken."

Die Welt of August 13 headlined their story on Berlin's impotence: "The Fears of the Powerful Faced with Deutsche Bank," and proceeded to quote an anonymous government source that nobody knows how bad Deutsche Bank's derivatives porfolio actually is. They report that when Finance Minister Wolfgang Schäuble was asked about the bank at the G-20 Finance Ministers meeting, he could only comment tersely, "I'm not saying anything about that."

"Nothing is stable in the European banking system," said Lyndon LaRouche in response on Aug. 17. "The German economy is on the edge of an explosion. Merkel and Schäuble are trying to manage the impossible. They must go. It's only a question of when the break will occur." Germany must make a decision to cast off the London and Wall Street-centered derivatives and related speculative toxic assets. Deutsche Bank competes for the top of the list of the 10 banks in London, which, as mutual counterparties, control over 92% of London's derivatives turnover,— which is in turn 46% of world derivatives turnover,—just among themselves! Way behind London, Wall Street and the United States come in with 24% (in 2011). This is what led the IMF to call Deutsche Bank the most dangerous bank in the world.

There is a means to solve this crisis, but only if leaders emerge immediately in Germany to restore stability. This requires, first, the recapitalization of Deutsche Bank under a new regime which writes off the worthless derivative bubble and restores commercial banking under Glass-Steagall-style regulation. Deutsche Bank must be returned to the policies of its former Chairman Alfred Herrhausen, murdered in 1989 by still-unidentified assassins. If that is done now, LaRouche said, then Germany, in cooperation with Putin's Russia, can avoid a sudden crash and drive a new paradigm of cooperation between the trans-Atlantic nations and the Russia-China partnership which is now leading the world economy forward, despite the Western collapse.

In her July 29 speech at the Chinese led G-20 Think Tank (T20) preparatory meeting in Beijing, Helga Zepp-LaRouche called for a global Glass-Steagall to be linked to the global adoption of the World Silk Road growth plan at the September G-20 Summit. As the European Union is dysfunctional, as the case of Deutsche Bank demonstrates, the responsibility and necessity rests now upon Germany to prevent a chaotic financial collapse and show the way of cooperation with Russia and China.

Who Was Alfred Herrhausen in 1989?

by David Cherry

Aug. 23—Deutsche Bank Chairman Alfred Herrhausen had a different conception of "universal banking"—one entirely opposite to that of the casino bankers of his day and ours. He was an industrial banker and, like others before him, such as Jürgen Ponto of Dresdner Bank, he thought of industrialization in faraway places. He planned to open bank branches in Eastern Europe and the Middle East. He had plans for a development bank in Poland and had responsibility for the bank's dealings with South Africa, then approaching the cusp of transition to majority rule.

In October 1988, he consummated a large loan to the Soviet Union, a loan of such significance that Chancellor Helmut Kohl and Foreign Minister Hans-Dietrich Genscher were on hand in Moscow for the celebration. Deutsche Bank had almost acquired the status of a government institution, and it had established promising working relationships in Moscow.

Herrhausen was a curious and creative thinker whose mind freely traversed science, music, philosophy, and religion—in violation of the dominant culture of specialization. Like the great leaders of history, he had confidence in his own power to reach the right decision, and did not look to his colleagues for agreement. At the same time, he reached out, beyond his profession, to people in other walks of life—often to those of more modest standing—to make their experience his own. Especially after his appointment as Co-Chairman in 1985 (he became sole Chairman in 1988) he came to see himself as a world-historical individual, responsible for the greater good—far greater than that of merely achieving profits for a bank—because he saw the potential good that Deutsche Bank could achieve.

When the Berlin Wall fell in November 1989, who would shape the future? Herrhausen, or the hyenas of the City of London and Wall Street—and their economic hitmen? Herrhausen was assassinated three weeks later.

It is fitting that Mozart's Requiem was performed at his memorial service.[1]

Herrhausen's campaign for debt relief for developing countries, beginning in 1987, described in the following article, exemplifies the work of this remarkable leader.

Herrhausen's Campaign For Third World Debt Relief

First published in the German newspaper Neue Solidarität *in Feb. 2005. It has been translated by* EIR.

In 1987 at the annual meeting of the International Monetary Fund and World Bank, Alfred Herrhausen, the CEO of Deutsche Bank, called for partial debt relief for the developing countries. He was not speaking behind closed doors, but before hundreds of business journalists at an international press conference.

We called it the "debt bomb": The foreign debt contracted in the 1970s by many developing countries had high interest rates, and multiplied rapidly and automatically. Soon the debtor countries had acquired more interest charges than the original debt, so the total debt grew and grew. Eventually this unsustainable system had to explode.

Herrhausen had seen this coming. Author Dieter Balkhausen, in his biography of Herrhausen, reports how he wanted to solve the debt crisis.[2] In August 1987, at the funeral of Werner Blessing—a Deutsche Bank director who had been involved in frantic crisis management of the debt explosion—Balkhausen and Herr-

---

1. This sketch draws upon Andreas Platthaus, *Alfred Herrhausen: Eine deutsche Karriere*, Rowohlt Berlin, 2006. Herrhausen has been the subject of recent articles in *EIR*, in the July 22 and Aug. 5 issues.
2. Dieter Balkhausen, *Alfred Herrhausen: Macht, Politik und Moral*, Econ Taschenbuch Verlag, 1992, cited in the EIRNA study, "Strategy of Tension. The Problems of Internal Security: Extremism, Terrorism, Organized Crime," Wiesbaden, June 1993.

hausen had a conversation. Herrhausen argued as follows:

"If the interest on the debt is not lowered and the debts are not in some way reduced, the situation will be like that of firms that go bankrupt, and from whom in any case only a small portion of the debt can be recovered. Either way, you never again see the greater part of the money; so it would be better to prevent the ruin of the debtor countries."

Balkhausen reports the rest of the conversation, putting Herrhausen's comments in italics:

Debtors and creditors are therefore closely linked to each other; they are sitting together on top of the tower of debt, and both must question themselves about their complicity; indeed, they must cross-examine themselves.

I ask Herrhausen about the responsibility of the governments in the industrialized nations, and then he comes out with these controversial conclusions:

Governments scarcely do anything; not in connection with this problem. Every head of state, every finance minister is thinking about his own debt burden.

Shouldn't our government exert constructive pressure on the U.S. government, because isn't it primarily the horrendous creditor positions of the U.S. banks vis-à-vis the Latin American countries that makes worldwide debt reduction for all the developing countries so difficult?

Yes, our government ought to! But it doesn't, because it does not want to strain German-American friendship. But if the Americans do not handle the situation in a more coherent and decisive way, then the whole process of controlling the debt will proceed too slowly, and the problems will necessarily and automatically run out of control.

And the United States is plunging itself into its own debt crisis due to its huge government debt. Isn't this even more dangerous than the debt crisis of the Third World?

Yes, it is a double debt crisis, which can endanger the industrialized countries themselves. Because they are dependent on the United States,

Dieter Balkhausen's 1990 biography of Herrhausen, subtitled, "Power, Politics, Morality."

due to of its economic and political supremacy—dependent on the constantly fluctuating value of the dollar on the world market. Therefore the Reagan administration must be compelled to do more to help the affected countries, because otherwise too little is being done, especially for the poorest of the poor countries in Africa.

I asked him pointedly, Isn't this global issue therefore essentially the problem of the United States?

In principle that's correct, because a bad policy in the most powerful nation affects the entire world, including us. Our mistakes can hardly affect the United States, but conversely, their mistakes can sorely affect the Federal Republic.

The IMF Press Conference

A month later, in September, Herrhausen flew to Washington for the IMF annual meeting, where he made public his proposal for partial debt relief. Balkhausen reports:

Herrhausen proposed that a partial debt moratorium be considered for the most deeply indebted countries. He did so at an international press conference attended by hundreds of business journalists and with his colleague in the Deutsche Bank executive, Wilhelm Christians, sitting next to him.

It seems that Herrhausen had carefully chosen where to do this. The traditional annual meeting of the World Bank and International Monetary Fund is the place where government officials and central bank governors customarily debate financial, currency, and economic matters, and thousands of bankers from all over the world come in search of business contacts.

Although the German banker shows courage, he handles the situation more spontaneously than according to a calculated plan with a fixed conception. What he described to me at the end of August as a major political issue, matures as a compulsion to act—in a meeting with the Mexican President, Miguel de la Madrid. The Mexican President had invited the internationally known banker for a talk in Mexico City. Herrhausen visits him there while the Washington conference is still going on. The President, whose government has fought for years for an improvement in borrowing conditions, points to the harsh conditionalities of the World Bank, the IMF, and the U.S. government (budget cuts, structural adjustments), which are demanded for rolling over existing debts and obtaining "fresh money," and he asks Herrhausen, "What, in your opinion, would happen in your country politically, if you were to impose a large cut in living standards on the citizens?"

Miguel de la Madrid, President of Mexico 1982-1998. At his request, Herrhausen flew to Mexico City in 1987 to discuss the unpayable debt of developing countries.

More than a decade after Balkhausen's biography appeared, in November 2002, the European cultural television channel ARTE broadcast a documentary on Herrhausen's assassination, in which former Mexican President de la Madrid himself reports on his meeting with Herrhausen in 1987: "I explained our situation to him, namely that the governments of indebted countries such as Mexico could no longer hang on without relief. I told him, it is worthwhile to keep the debtor countries alive, because a dead debtor cannot pay."

Then the documentary quotes Herrhausen himself: "Then it crossed my mind that here we had to choose a different approach, and that it is probably inevitable that banks make certain sacrifices to help these countries. From the outset, there were two possible victims of the crisis: the creditor banks and the debtors. That is still true, but the power of the banks is now greater, and that of the debtors has diminished."

The Synarchist Reaction

Balkhausen also thinks that Herrhausen's conversation with the Mexican President had tipped the balance for his public drive for debt relief:

> Herrhausen, whose concern for the commonweal of our republic had often been evident, finds it impossible to avoid taking the debt issue head on, after his discussion with de la Madrid. Having returned to Washington, he uses the press conference to make his proposal, without suspecting, however, what would follow.

Even while still in Washington, Herrhausen

feels the air became leaden. At least, somewhat menacing thoughts easily come over him, as when a couple of months later he describes the ensuing frenzy in the banking community to a group of American and English journalists in Gütersloh (invited by the Bertelsmann Foundation) thus: "Take the next helicopter and get out of Washington; they will shoot you here."

His colleague Christians distances himself when he feels the cold headwind. The German bankers, who quickly signal their opposition, are just as furious as the American, English, and Japanese bankers.

In the ARTE documentary, Hilmar Kopper, one of Herrhausen's successors, expressed his opinion of Herrhausen's proposal for cancelling debt, with sarcasm: "Herrhausen said that if you waive all or parts of these obligations, then they don't exist anymore, and the problem is solved. That was a typically intellectual remark, namely to say that if we go through all of this in theory, we can eliminate the problem by eliminating the source of the problem." This earned for Herrhausen "the insanely huge support of the aging, careerist radicals of the 1968 era. They were all for debt obliteration. But it was not their money. That was the money of the evil banks, which can be annihilated without a thought. It was their own [the bankers'] fault that they extended credit to the Brazilians."

Why did Alfred Herrhausen think and act so unlike the majority of his colleagues at home and abroad? Could he perhaps have empathized more with the fate of ordinary people, because he himself was not "born with a silver spoon in his mouth"? Another biographer, Arthur P. Schmidt, wrote, "Alfred Herrhausen, who was born in Essen in 1930 and identified himself as a 'child of the Ruhr,' belonged to the generation that experienced the post-war period. Because he came from a family of modest means, he had to earn his tuition for his business studies as a mineworker."[3]

---

3. Arthur P. Schmidt, "Alfred Herrhausen: Vorbild mit Visionen," *Q-Magazin*, 4/95. The Ruhr is a major European center of coal mining and steel production.

www.ingramcontent.com/pod-product-compliance
Lightning Source LLC
Chambersburg PA
CBHW051953280526
45789CB00009B/3268